Who Was Charles Schulz?

by Joan Holub

illustrated by Tim Foley

Penguin Workshop

For Paul Holub, a Snoopy fan.
A huge thank-you to super-smart
Jane O'Connor—JH

For Kirk Rose, my first "drawing buddy"—TF

PENGUIN WORKSHOP
An imprint of Penguin Random House LLC, New York

First published in the United States of America by Penguin Workshop,
an imprint of Penguin Random House LLC, New York, 2022

Text copyright © 2022 by Joan Holub
Illustrations copyright © 2022 by Penguin Random House LLC

PENGUIN is a registered trademark and PENGUIN WORKSHOP is a trademark
of Penguin Books Ltd. WHO HQ & Design is a registered trademark
of Penguin Random House LLC.

Visit us online at penguinrandomhouse.com.

Library of Congress Control Number: 2021049002

Printed in the United States of America

ISBN 9780451532541 (paperback)   10 9 8 7 6 5 4 3 2 1 WOR
ISBN 9780451532565 (library binding) 10 9 8 7 6 5 4 3 2 1 WOR

Contents

Who Was Charles Schulz?

In his first week of kindergarten, Charles Schulz already proved what a good artist he was. When the teacher gave the kids in the class paper and crayons, they all lay on the floor to draw. Charles drew a picture of a man shoveling snow, with a palm tree in the background.

It was a funny idea. But he wasn't satisfied with his picture. The shovel didn't look right, but he didn't know how to fix it.

Still, when his teacher saw his drawing, she told him, "Someday, Charles, you're going to be an artist."

By age six, Charles had decided he wanted to be a cartoonist. He would grow up to create one of the most popular comic strips ever—*Peanuts!* Its cast of beloved characters includes Charlie Brown, Snoopy, Lucy, Linus, Schroeder, Pigpen, Sally, Woodstock, Peppermint Patty, and more.

Of all his characters, Charlie Brown was most like Charles. Both were ordinary kids who didn't stand out in a crowd. Like Charlie Brown, Charles could be quiet and shy.

Charles Schulz seemed like a relaxed and happy guy. Inside, however, he was often anxious and worried, even after he became rich and famous. But when he was drawing comics, he felt confident and in charge. He loved his job.

A *Peanuts* comic strip

Millions of people grew up reading *Peanuts*. Surprisingly, Charles had wanted to name his comic strip something else!

CHAPTER 1
A Boy Called Sparky

Charles M. Schulz was born in Minneapolis, Minnesota, on November 26, 1922. His uncle soon nicknamed him Sparky after Spark Plug. Spark Plug was the horse in the popular *Barney Google* comic strip. The name stuck. All his life, Charles's friends and family would call him Sparky.

Barney Google and Spark Plug

Sparky was an only child. He grew up in Saint Paul, a city right next to Minneapolis, with his mom, Dena, and his dad, Carl. Carl owned the Family Barbershop, and they lived nearby.

Sparky was proud of his dad and liked to hang out at the barbershop. When Sparky's hair grew long, Carl would cut it. But if a customer

came into the shop, Sparky had to move aside. He'd wait around with half a haircut till the customer left. That was kind of embarrassing!

TVs weren't around then. Like most families, the Schulzes listened to radio programs. They had to imagine what all the characters in a series looked like and in their minds "see" the action happening.

Comics were super popular. Both grown-ups and kids loved them. People spent hours reading the funny papers. That was what the comic strip pages in newspapers were called.

Sparky and his dad would read comics together and discuss them. *What will happen in next week's strips?* they'd wonder.

In elementary school, Sparky was a good student. He was so smart that he got to skip half of the third and fifth grades. He always carried a pencil in his pocket and was great at copying comic characters like Popeye and Mickey Mouse. Other kids asked him to make pictures in their notebooks. At home, he sometimes drew on the cardboard that came inside his dad's shirts from the laundry because paper was expensive.

Early US Comics

In 1895, a colorful comic strip called *The Yellow Kid* by Richard Outcault appeared in the *New York World* newspaper. It was one of the first newspaper strips in the United States, and starred a barefoot boy in a long yellow shirt. At that time, newspapers would try almost anything to get more readers. Some would even write interesting headlines that weren't altogether true! That kind of trickery was nicknamed "yellow journalism" after *The Yellow Kid*. The *New York Journal* introduced *The Katzenjammer Kids* comic strip by Rudolph Dirks in 1897. It starred prankster twin brothers named Hans

Main character from
The Yellow Kid

and Fritz. *Little Nemo in Slumberland* by Winsor McCay appeared in the *New York Herald* in 1905. It was about a boy who visited amazing places in his dreams. Sometimes his bed grew legs and walked around. It's considered one of the most magical comics ever published. In 1938, *Superman*, created by Jerry Siegel and Joe Shuster, became one of the first super-popular superheroes to star in comics.

For his eleventh birthday, Sparky bought himself a book called *How to Draw Cartoons* by Clare Briggs. He kept practicing and learning.

Sparky often felt lonely without brothers or sisters. He'd go visit his friend Shermy, who lived around the corner. Sparky liked to listen to Shermy's mom play classical music on her piano. On Saturday afternoons, the boys would go to movie theaters to see short films called serials.

On Sundays, the Schulzes sometimes visited Sparky's mom's family at their farm. His cousins were noisy, played rough, and sometimes teased him. He was a shy city boy. Cows and other farm animals seemed scary. He didn't enjoy the trips.

Minnesota had long snowy winters. Kids in Saint Paul would skate on ponds or on patches of ice that formed on sidewalks or streets. Sometimes Sparky's dad hosed down their yard.

The water would freeze into a skating rink perfect for ice hockey. Kids in the neighborhood liked to come over to skate at the Schulzes'. One of Sparky's favorite books was *Hans Brinker; or,*

The Silver Skates by Mary Mapes Dodge. It was about a boy and his sister who try to win a pair of skates in an ice-skating race.

Sparky enjoyed sports and often forgot

his shyness in his desire to win. In spring and summer, he played baseball. These were just pickup games. There was no organized Little League back then. (It began in 1939.)

One summer, something exciting happened. A playground supervisor noticed how much Sparky and his friends enjoyed baseball. He

started a league for them with four teams, playing two days a week. Not only was Sparky chosen as a team manager, he switched off playing catcher and pitcher. Even though the games didn't start until 9:00 a.m., he would arrive at 8:30 with the equipment. His dedication paid off. His team won the season championship!

CHAPTER 2
A Love of Drawing

One day, Sparky's parents took him to the library to see an exhibit of comic strips. Many were by famous cartoonists. For the first time, he got to study original hand-drawn comics up close.

A series of boxes called panels had become the usual format for comics. The row or rows of panels were called a strip. The action started in the first panel and continued in the panels that followed. Cartoonists would draw stars to indicate an injury, like a skinned knee, and curvy lines to show action like running. They added sound-effect words like *Eek!* and *Ka-pow!*, and drew bubbles to contain thoughts or speech.

Editors' notes were penciled around the edges of the comics in the exhibit. Sparky could see where mistakes had been corrected. Cartoons went through many revisions, he realized. They weren't perfect right off. He thought these comics were way better than his own. He went home, tore up his drawings, and started new ones.

The Schulz family got a black-and-white dog named Spike when Sparky was thirteen. This dog was so smart, he could understand fifty words, ring the doorbell, and fetch potatoes from the cellar. Sparky's dad wrote a list of weird, dangerous things Spike had eaten.

Perspective and Composition

Artists often take classes to learn many techniques, some of which include composition and perspective. Composition means how things in a picture are arranged. Good composition usually includes a focal point that attracts your attention. Perspective is a way of making a two-dimensional

picture seem three-dimensional. In a technique called two-point perspective, lines slant toward vanishing points placed on the horizon line. This makes some parts of the picture appear near, and others farther away. If an object in a picture is big, it will appear closer to the viewer than a smaller one. Making an object overlap another can also make it seem closer.

Sparky's dad sent it to a newspaper with a picture of Spike that Sparky had drawn. The list and drawing were printed in Robert Ripley's popular newspaper cartoon *Believe It or Not!*

Sparky's drawing in Ripley's *Believe It or Not!*

It was the very first time Sparky's art was published! He was fourteen years old.

Sparky often didn't make good grades as a teenager. Skipping a grade back in elementary school meant he was younger and smaller than his high-school classmates. He was too shy to talk to girls or go on dates. Bigger kids sometimes bullied him. He felt like he didn't fit in. So maybe that's why he didn't try very hard at schoolwork.

Near the end of Sparky's high school years, his grades improved. A teacher asked him to draw some cartoons for the yearbook. How exciting! When the yearbooks came out, he checked every page. His drawings weren't there. This was a huge letdown. He never found out why they weren't included. Throughout his life, he never got over similar disappointments.

Something good, however, happened during his last year of high school. His mom showed him a newspaper ad for the Federal Schools program. It was a home-study correspondence school that taught art skills, including cartooning.

"Do You Like to Draw?" the ad's headline

asked. Yes! Sparky *did* like to draw. He began taking classes from the Federal Schools program in February 1940, at age seventeen. Right away, the art school mailed him a box of materials to use for his assignments.

There were no computers or online schools in those days. Sparky and other students drew by hand and mailed their art homework to the school. In reply, a teacher would place a sheet of tracing paper over a student's drawing, and then write notes on it with arrows pointing to what needed improvement. Teachers also suggested ways to create realistic shading. The assignment and teacher's advice would then be mailed back to each student. Sparky also learned about what to do to make a career of drawing comics. He needed to send proper business letters to companies he hoped might buy his comics. So he bought a used typewriter and taught himself to type.

Sparky could have enrolled in a different art school where he attended classes in person, but he chose not to. Unsure of his talent, he didn't want to risk being embarrassed when his work was criticized by teachers face-to-face.

The Federal Schools course cost $170, paid in $10 monthly payments. That was a lot of money in 1940. Haircuts cost only twenty-five cents at Sparky's dad's barber shop, so his family was far from rich. When payments were sometimes late to the art school, Sparky worried he'd be kicked out. But owing money wasn't unusual in those days. The Great Depression had begun in 1929. Nevertheless, Sparky's dad paid the school bills, and Sparky graduated in 1941.

After graduation, Sparky needed to get a job, but it was impossible for him to get one making comics right away. For a while, he worked at a grocery store and made home deliveries. He didn't like delivering groceries because people's dogs barked at him. One of his next jobs was sweeping floors and stacking paper at a printing company. When he drew a picture of a man who worked the printing press, the pressman really liked it. That made Sparky feel great.

All his life, he would recall happy moments like that when someone praised his art.

The Great Depression

In October 1929, the US stock market crashed. When stock prices suddenly dropped way down and didn't rise again, banks failed. That meant people lost all the money they had saved. By 1933, one-fourth of the adults in the United States didn't have a job and couldn't find one. Millions were homeless. Sometimes people stood in long lines hoping to get free food for their families. Farms and companies went out of business at a record rate. The rest of the world was in financial trouble, too. There have been economic hard times in the United States and other countries since then, but none have been as bad. The Great Depression ended around 1939.

In his spare time, Sparky kept on improving his drawing skills. He tried to sell his cartoons to popular magazines like *Collier's* and *The Saturday Evening Post*. He got rejected every time. It was frustrating.

His parents, however, were proud of his illustrations and supported his dream. A successful cartoonist could earn a lot of money. But they were a little worried his dream might not work out. Then what would become of him?

CHAPTER 3
War and Work

At age twenty, Sparky was drafted into the US Army to fight in World War II. He would have to put his dream of becoming a cartoonist on hold.

Before he left for training camp, his mom bid him a very sad goodbye. She had cancer. They knew they'd probably never see each other again. Just days after he left, his mom died. Sparky was heartbroken. One of his biggest regrets in life was that she never got to see his success.

Military training at Camp Campbell in Kentucky was a lonely, unhappy time for Sparky. Even though he made friends, he missed his mother a lot and didn't like being away from home. For pleasure, he drew pictures in his sketchbook of everyday life at the camp.

World War II

World War II began on September 1, 1939, when Hitler's German army invaded Poland. Adolf Hitler wanted to conquer all of Europe. In response, France and Great Britain declared war on Germany. Japan was on the side of Germany. In the beginning, the United States tried to stay out of the fight. But then, on December 7, 1941, that changed.

Japanese airplanes attacked US Navy ships in Pearl Harbor, Hawaii. The next day, the United States entered World War II, with troops fighting both in Europe and the Pacific. On May 7, 1945, Nazi Germany officially surrendered. In early August, the United States dropped an atomic bomb on each of the Japanese cities of Hiroshima and Nagasaki. Japan surrendered on September 2, 1945. At last World War II was over.

Sparky admired the comics that Bill Mauldin drew in the *Stars and Stripes,* a US military newspaper. Many soldiers enjoyed Mauldin's Willie and Joe characters. They were funny at times but also showed the danger soldiers faced in wartime.

Sparky became a staff sergeant in his division and a machine-gun squad leader. In early 1945, he was sent to fight in France, then moved on to Germany. He was awarded a special combat badge. In August that year, he sailed back to the United States. The war was almost over.

After the war, Sparky returned to Saint Paul to live with his dad above the barbershop. He was more determined than ever to become a published comic strip artist.

In March 1946, he got a job lettering the words in comic strips for a company that created religious teaching materials. Someone else did the drawings. He became really fast and good at lettering. Later, that came in handy for writing speech balloons in *Peanuts*.

That summer, he was hired to teach at the Art Instruction Schools. It was the same program (with a new name) where he had taken classes. The job paid $32 a week. That was a good salary back then.

The job turned out to be great for him. All

day, he worked at a desk in a big room surrounded by ten or so other talented teachers. When students sent their drawing assignments to the school, Sparky reviewed them and made suggestions for improvement. At night, he continued doing his lettering job.

Sparky liked working at the school. He and the other teachers joked around. They played card games at lunch. Sometimes someone would start whistling the beginning of a song. Then someone else would whistle the next part, and so on until the whole song had been whistled by the group.

Some of the other teachers were struggling artists, too. Sparky showed them his comic strips, and they gave him advice. He did the same for them. They learned from one another and helped each other improve.

His fellow instructors included people named Charlie Brown, Linus Maurer, and Frieda Rich. Do those names sound familiar? Sparky named

Sparky shows the real Charlie Brown his character Charlie Brown

Peanuts characters after them. When he first drew his Linus character, he showed it to Linus Maurer, who gave him feedback.

In February 1947, something great happened for Sparky. His work got published in a comic book for the very first time! The full-color page of four separate panel cartoons titled *Just Keep Laughing* came out in a religious publication called *Topix*. Did the characters he drew look like the ones in *Peanuts*? No. Not yet.

Later that year, the *Minneapolis Star Tribune* newspaper published two of his comics called *Li'l Folks*. Soon the *St. Paul Pioneer Press* would begin publishing more *Li'l Folks* comics once a week. Things were looking up for Sparky.

The logo for Sparky's *Li'l Folks* strip

CHAPTER 4
Selling Comics

Sparky worked at the art school for five years. Meanwhile, he kept improving his drawing and polishing his comic art style. Every chance he got, he would show his comics to magazine and newspaper companies, hoping they'd buy them.

Walt Disney Studios, 1947

Sometimes he mailed his cartoons. Sometimes he would show them in person. He even tried to sell his work to Disney. No luck. He kept getting rejected. Later, Disney Studios would offer him a tryout for a job with them, but he said no. He wanted to draw his own characters, and so kept trying to make it on his own.

On May 29, 1948, a one-panel cartoon he created was published in the *Saturday Evening Post*. This was a big deal! The *Pioneer Press* was a local paper, but the *Evening Post* was a national magazine! The *Post* would publish sixteen more of his cartoons. In one comic, two kids wear sailor hats while sitting in a round pan that's floating in a large bathtub. One looks ahead and says, "We must be approaching civilization . . . I can see my mother!"

The characters in the *Post* were not as detailed

and realistic as those in the *Pioneer* had been. More and more, his kids were starting to resemble those that would star in *Peanuts*.

The *Pioneer* and *Post* sales had been nice. Still, what Sparky most wanted was his own syndicated comic strip featuring the same characters over and over. Syndication meant that each comic strip he drew would be published in many different newspapers all over the country. With syndication, the money added up.

In 1949, when Sparky was twenty-seven years old, he mailed samples of his *Li'l Folks* comics to United Feature Syndicate in New York. Fingers crossed!

Comics Syndication

Companies called syndicates sell the rights to reproduce comics and cartoons. Newspapers, magazines, and other markets worldwide rely on syndicates to supply them with ready-made strips. Because the same comic strip gets sold to many markets, a cartoonist can earn more money and reach a bigger audience. The cartoonist and syndicate often split the money equally. In the early days of syndication, a deal might mean that the syndicate owned the characters in a comic strip. The syndicate could hire another artist to continue the comics if the original creator died or quit.

For weeks he awaited a reply. United Feature was a big syndicate. It received over a thousand submissions each year and might accept only one. The odds were against him. Finally Sparky got a reply. The syndicate wanted him to come to its office for a meeting. Was this the break he'd been hoping for?

Sparky took a train to New York City. He didn't go empty-handed. He brought more new comic strips he'd been working on. In one, a boy gives a girl a bite of his ice-cream cone. She spits it out, surprised. It's mashed potato, not ice cream!

The syndicate liked his comics! It gave him a five-year contract. He and the syndicate would split the profits from his comics equally. Sparky's dream was coming true.

Just one problem. His *Li'l Folks* title was similar to the title of two other comic strips.

So the syndicate decided Sparky's strip needed a new name. He suggested calling it *Good Ol' Charlie Brown* or *Charlie Brown*. The syndicate, however, decided on *Peanuts*. *The Howdy Doody Show* on TV was very popular with kids at that time.

The Howdy Doody Show plays on TV

Their audience was known as the Peanut Gallery. Maybe this was where the idea to call Sparky's comic strip *Peanuts* came from. Or maybe it was because his characters were small and cute like peanuts!

What did Sparky think of the new name? He didn't like it one bit. He didn't even understand what it meant. Later on, he decided it probably didn't matter what the strip was called. He was just glad readers liked it.

On October 2, 1950, the first *Peanuts* comic strip appeared in seven newspapers including the *Washington Post* and the *Seattle Daily Times*. It was four panels. It showed kids named Patty (not the same as Peppermint Patty) and Shermy (named after Sparky's childhood friend) sitting on

a sidewalk. As Charlie Brown walks by, Shermy calls him good ol' Charlie Brown. Later, Shermy admits to Patty that he hates him. In Sparky's early strips, characters were sometimes snarkier than in later ones.

Sparky earned ninety dollars for his first month of strips. They ran Monday through Saturday in black and white. *Peanuts* was not an instant hit. In its first year, it came in last in the *New York World Telegram*'s reader survey ranking of cartoons. The strip needed to sell to a hundred newspapers to be considered a success. So far, *Peanuts* had sold to only thirty-six.

Sparky once compared his comic strip to a piano. With many keys, a piano can make beautiful music. With many characters, he could always think up an interesting story for one of them each day. But there were so many characters that readers couldn't tell them apart. The answer to the problem was giving each character one or more tags. A tag identified the character right away. It might be an object they owned (Linus's blanket) or a personality trait (Lucy was bossy).

For a while, *Peanuts* stayed a black-and-white comic Monday through Saturday. On January 6, 1952, a color strip also began running on Sundays.

Book of *Peanuts* comics published in 1952

That same year, some of Sparky's newspaper comics were reprinted in a book titled *Peanuts*. This helped the comic strip reach new fans. In time, the *Peanuts* characters became known around the world.

CHAPTER 5
Charlie Brown and Lucy

Sometimes Sparky doodled to come up with ideas for a strip. Once he had a good one, he sketched it with pencil. He would work fast, afraid that he might forget his idea before he could put it on paper. He tried his characters in different poses and moved them around inside a panel to see what worked best. He might write reminders to himself around the edges of the page.

He didn't bother making detailed sketches. He knew his characters so well that he could ink them perfectly atop a pencil sketch. This way of working helped keep his drawing fresh and energetic. He used a pen tipped with a metal point called a nib. He would dip the nib end of his pen in black India ink over and over as he drew the final comic. It took him ten minutes to an hour to draw a black and white daily strip. Colorful Sunday ones took longer. For those, he would use a numbered color chart to tell the printshop which colors to add where. Drawing a comic strip was hard work. But it was fun, too.

Even though he was his own boss, Sparky tried not to let anyone down. He met deadlines, usually finishing his comics four to six weeks ahead of time.

Although Sparky named some of his *Peanuts* characters after friends, most of the characters were actually like *him* in some way. He was a lot like Charlie Brown, the star of the comic strip. Charlie Brown and Sparky both owned dogs. Both of their dads were barbers. Both were sensitive and could get hurt feelings. Both played football and baseball. Sparky once played a baseball game that his team lost 40 to 0. So did Charlie Brown.

Like Charlie Brown, Sparky was a worrier. Sometimes he worried so much he got a stomachache. The more famous *Peanuts* got, the more people wanted Sparky to travel to make speeches or do interviews. But traveling anywhere made him anxious.

Sparky didn't like worrying so much. Still, he wondered what might happen if he ever became a truly happy person. Would his comics still be good? He wasn't so sure. What if his humor sprang out of his unhappy feelings and experiences? Like being lonely or being bossed around.

His *Peanuts* character Lucy is *very* bossy. She thinks she's an expert on everything. At her lemonade stand, she sells advice for five cents. She believes in girl power and wants to be a president or a queen. There's a lot to admire about her, but sometimes she can be a bit mean.

In a famous ongoing *Peanuts* gag, Lucy holds a football ready for Charlie Brown to kick. He runs up. Surprise! Lucy pulls the football away, and Charlie Brown kicks empty air, does a flip, and falls on the ground. As a boy, Sparky held the football for other kids at kickoff. He'd often been tempted to whip the ball away at the last minute as a practical joke.

Sometimes readers wrote to Sparky asking him to please let Charlie Brown succeed in kicking the football Lucy held. At least once!

But Sparky never did. He avoided ending ongoing gags such as that one. He thought that doing so might ruin the basic structure of his comic strip.

Even when Sparky got mad, he did not use curse words. Instead he might say something like "good grief." Charlie Brown became known for saying that or groaning, "AAUGH!"

Despite their problems, Sparky and Charlie Brown both remained hopeful. Charlie Brown's baseball team always loses. Yet he keeps hoping it might win. Whenever Charlie Brown tries to fly a kite, it gets stuck in a tree. But he tries again another day. No matter how many times Lucy pulls away the football, he still goes for it. He always hopes *this* time will be different. No matter how many times Sparky's comics got rejected by publishers, he kept trying and hoping until he got published. And it worked!

CHAPTER 6
Everything I Am

Sparky once said, "If you read the strip, you would know me. Everything I am goes into the strip." If he was happy about something one day, he might create a comic about Charlie Brown's little sister Sally being happy. If Sparky was worried about something, Charlie Brown might be worried.

Of all the *Peanuts* characters, Charlie Brown's beagle, Snoopy, was probably the favorite among fans. Sparky's childhood dog, Spike, was the inspiration for him. Snoopy almost got named Sniffy, but Sparky found out another comic was already using that name. Then he remembered that his mom had once said that if they got another dog, it should be named Snoopy. Snoopy it was!

Since Sparky had done poorly in high school, he knew how getting a bad grade could make you feel. Peppermint Patty makes a D-minus on every school test. She has freckles and wears sandals. Like Sparky, she's good at sports and loves to win.

Peppermint Patty and her friend Marcie both have crushes on Charlie Brown, but he never figures that out. Although Sparky got crushes on girls, he was often too shy to talk to them. He understood how it felt if someone didn't notice you. He had a knack for creating gently funny stories involving universal emotions—the kinds of feelings people can relate to. Like not being the best, making bad grades, being teased, or wanting what you can't have.

While working at the Art Instruction Schools, Sparky dated a woman named Donna Johnson. She had red hair and blue eyes. He was heartbroken

Charles Schulz with Donna Johnson

when she married someone else. Donna was the main inspiration for the Little Red-Haired Girl in *Peanuts*. Charlie Brown dreams of the Little Red-Haired girl liking him but is too shy to speak to her.

The character Pigpen shows us that it's cool to be different. He is messy and surrounded by a dirt cloud. Pigpen doesn't care if anybody is bothered by it. He likes to say, "I'm a dust magnet!" Readers loved Pigpen, but Sparky had a hard time thinking of story ideas for him. So Pigpen appears in only about a hundred comics.

Lucy has one soft spot. A boy named Schroeder. All he wants to do is play music on his toy piano. Sparky was that way, too—with comics. There was nothing he enjoyed more than creating his strip. His favorite classical music composer was Brahms. He chose Beethoven, however, to be Schroeder's favorite because he thought the name Beethoven sounded funnier.

Ludwig van Beethoven

CHAPTER 7
Good Times, Bad Times

In 1951, Sparky met Joyce Steele Halverson at a party with some of his art school friends. They both enjoyed music, and she was energetic and lots of fun. If Sparky felt like being quiet around others, he could count on Joyce

Sparky and Joyce at their wedding

to do the talking. Some people thought they saw bits of Joyce in Lucy's outspoken personality.

Sparky and Joyce got married on April 18, 1951. He adopted Joyce's one-year-old daughter, Meredith. At first, the three of them lived with his dad and his dad's new wife in a small Saint Paul apartment. It was crowded, so Sparky drew his comic strips sitting at a table in the basement.

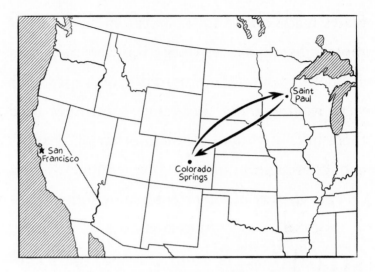

Joyce wanted to move to Colorado Springs, so they did. But their new home was small. And, with a new family around, it still wasn't easy for Sparky to concentrate on his work. So he rented an office downtown. He really missed his dad and the friends he'd left behind in Saint Paul. After nine months in Colorado, he and his family, that now included baby Monte, moved back there.

By 1955, *Peanuts* was in one hundred newspapers. At last! By 1956, Sparky was earning $4,000 a month. Most families in the United

States made only $4,800 a year at the time. As more of Sparky's newspaper strips were published as books, *Peanuts'* fame spread. College students were reading them. Professors sometimes used them in courses about human behavior. Sparky's comics brought in more and more money.

Peanuts was different from most other well-known comics of the time. *Prince Valiant* and *Dick Tracy* were more serious and contained lots of words. There was plenty of detail and action. The characters were grown-ups. *Peanuts* was gentle, amusing, and uncluttered. It stood out. Adults were occasionally mentioned, but were never shown. When asked why that was, Sparky joked that grown-ups were too tall to fit inside the

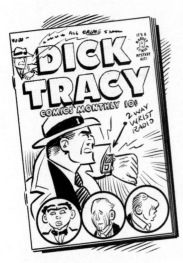

Dick Tracy comic book from 1952

panels. The truth was, he just didn't think adults belonged in the kid world he had created.

In addition to Joyce's daughter Meredith, and Monte, Sparky's family would grow to include three more children, Craig, Amy, and Jill. Surrounded by kids, he knew what they were like. Some of them cuddled blankets when they were little. That's why he gave Lucy's little brother, Linus, a security blanket. (That's a term for a comforting object that *Peanuts* made famous.)

Sparky, Joyce, and their five children

It was hard raising kids in Minnesota. During the long cold winters, coats, boots, and mittens had to go on every time the five children went outside.

In 1958, Sparky and his family decided to move to the warmer climate of Sebastopol, near San Francisco, California. By then, they could afford a really nice house on twenty-eight acres of land. It had apple orchards, tennis courts,

Sparky's home in Sebastopol

a nine-hole miniature golf course with a waterfall and small castle, a pool, and horses to ride. And there was already a photographer's studio on the property where Sparky could do his cartooning work!

Like his dad, Sparky was a hard worker. He liked having a regular routine. He worked in his studio Monday through Friday from about 9:00 a.m. to 4:00 p.m. For lunch, he usually had the same thing every day—a ham sandwich, milk, and pudding. His daughter Amy later recalled that he always made time for his kids. He liked having them hang out in his studio

Sparky's daily lunch

after school. Sparky played sports with them and did regular dad things like driving his daughter Jill to ice-skating competitions.

By 1958, *Peanuts* was in 395 newspapers. Sparky got lots of fan mail and tried to answer every letter, but that eventually became impossible. By 1967, he was getting five hundred letters a week. Some were from famous movie and TV stars like Shirley Temple and Carol Burnett!

CHAPTER 8
Changes

It's common for an artist's style to change as they grow older—whether it's a famous painter like Pablo Picasso or a comic strip artist. The *Peanuts* characters slowly changed over the years. If you compare the early comic strips to later ones, you can spot differences. Charlie Brown's face got rounder and his nose and ears got bigger. His shirt was plain in the first comic. A black zigzag stripe appeared on it about two and a half months later in the December 21, 1950 strip. Some of the characters' personalities changed and they also grew older, but they always remained kids. Charlie Brown was four years old in the beginning. By 1979, he was eight and a half. And that was the age he stayed.

50s   70s   90s

Snoopy's character design evolved over the years

Snoopy changed more than any other character. He made his first appearance in the third *Peanuts* comic strip. He trotted across four panels while a girl watered flowers, including one growing from his head. Snoopy's nose started out pointed. Later his head became more peanut shaped. At first, Snoopy walked on four legs like a real dog. In a 1957 strip, Charlie Brown decided to train him to walk on two legs. To his dismay, Snoopy was instantly good at it. From then on, Snoopy walked on two legs. This allowed the dog to act more humanlike.

Snoopy got a typewriter and began typing stories atop his doghouse in 1965. That beagle began to dream big. He imagined himself as different heroes. He became a wartime flying ace on the roof of his doghouse, chasing a pilot called the Red Baron. He even beat the astronauts to the moon! At least, he did in his imagination. Still, Snoopy never spoke like the human characters. Readers just saw his thoughts.

Snoopy was lots of fun and the character Sparky most wished to be like. In fact, he would get so many ideas for Snoopy that Sparky had to be careful not to let Snoopy take over the comic strip!

Sparky studied the sketchbooks from his army days to help write the Red Baron chases. Recalling being in military training camp also inspired camping experiences for the kids in *Peanuts*.

The Red Baron

The Red Baron was the nickname of the real German fighter pilot Manfred von Richthofen. He fought against the United States and its allies during World War I. For two years, he commanded a group of pilots with bright-colored fighter planes known as the Flying Circus. His red triplane, daring flying style, and record of shooting down eighty enemy aircraft made him infamous. In 1918, he was killed in a dogfight (a military aircraft battle) at age twenty-five.

In one comic, Linus and Charlie Brown are cheering because school has let out for the summer. Then Lucy announces that the boys have to go to summer camp. The last panel of the comic strip shows Charlie Brown and Linus on the bus to camp, both looking very disappointed.

Sparky never forgot the brave soldiers he'd met during World War II. He would often create a comic strip to honor them on Veteran's Day. In one comic, Snoopy toasts *Stars and Stripes* cartoonist Bill Mauldin with a mug of root beer.

Bill Mauldin

There were other things Sparky especially enjoyed drawing. Like Linus's wild hair. He liked to draw rain, so it was fun for him to create a scene where a baseball game got rained out.

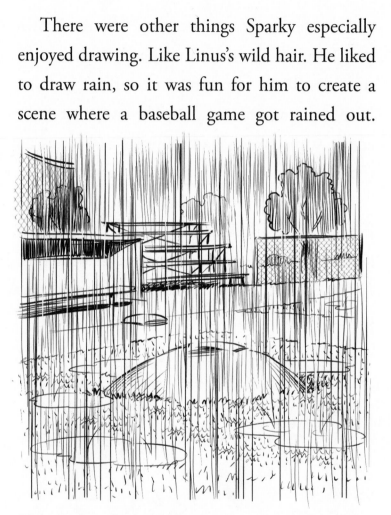

Not so fun for Charlie Brown, who sometimes refused to accept a rain-out and insisted that his team keep playing!

Snowmen were also fun for Sparky. In one wintry cartoon, Snoopy befriended a snowman. Though he begged the sun to spare his icy friend, the snowman melted. It's a funny comic, but also a reminder of  how much we miss a friend or loved one who is gone. Sparky was heartbroken when his mom died. Perhaps his feelings of loss inspired that comic strip.

Now and then, he added new characters to *Peanuts*. A small yellow bird that sometimes flew upside down appeared in 1967. He became Snoopy's friend. Later Sparky would name him Woodstock after the 1969 outdoor rock music festival in upstate New York. A new Black character named Franklin appeared in 1968.

Harriet Glickman and Franklin

On April 4, 1968, Black civil rights leader Martin Luther King Jr. was assassinated in Memphis, Tennessee. It was a terrible moment in US history. His famous "I Have a Dream" speech had called for equal rights for Black people. He hoped Black children and white children could become good friends. A teacher named Harriet Glickman hoped there was some way to keep Dr. King's dream alive. There were hardly any Black characters in ads, movies, or TV shows of that time. There weren't any in *Peanuts*, either. She wrote a letter to Charles Schulz on April 15, 1968. Harriet wondered if adding a Black character to the popular comic strip could help change things. Sparky wanted to help. On July 31, 1968, a Black boy named Franklin appeared in *Peanuts*. In the strip, Franklin returns Charlie Brown's missing beach ball, and the boys hang out together. In true *Peanuts* style, this strip was simple and gentle, yet powerful. It was about friendship as Dr. King dreamed of. Franklin would later appear in many more *Peanuts* comic strips, animated TV specials, and films.

CHAPTER 9
Happiness Is . . .

In 1962, Charles Schulz published a book called *Happiness Is a Warm Puppy*. It included sayings that began "Happiness is . . ." alongside illustrations of *Peanuts* characters. It was about the simple pleasures that make people happy.

The book hit the *New York Times* best-seller list for forty-five weeks! Sparky drew all the pictures in this book. As he got busier, other artists were hired to help draw some of his comic books.

Things were going well. So well that it seemed a good time to make the first *Peanuts* animated TV special. Sparky met with two talented friends, Bill Melendez and Lee Mendelson, to discuss ideas for a script, which Sparky would write.

Back in elementary school, Sparky had been in a Christmas pageant. He and other students had each held one large letter to spell out the words *MERRY CHRISTMAS*. The kids before him spoke their lines quietly in turn. When his turn

came, he held up his letter—*A*—and boomed out: "*A* stands for all of us!" Someone in the audience laughed, which embarrassed him. All kinds of things could go haywire in a children's play. Which might make a fun TV show!

Sparky wanted the show to focus on the true meaning of Christmas. Most comedy shows included the sounds of fake laughter so viewers at home would think that something was funny. Sparky decided not to include a laugh track. Usually adult actors did the voices in cartoons, pretending to be kids. Sparky used mostly real kids for the voices. For Charlie Brown, he and the show's producers wanted a blah-sounding voice. The girl playing Lucy was chosen because her voice sounded somewhat crabby. The boy playing Linus had a lisp.

In the TV special, Charlie Brown feels sad at Christmas. Others around him act as if the holiday is only about getting gifts. He wonders what Christmas really means. The answer comes from Linus, who tells the story of the birth of Jesus from the Bible. Sparky thought it was important to include this. He enjoyed reading about religion and discussing his beliefs.

Although Linus is a little kid, he is often wise. So he was a good choice to get across a message of peace and goodwill. In the show, he inspires the other characters to join in an act of kindness. They decorate Charlie Brown's droopy, skinny fir tree until it sparkles.

When TV executives saw a preview, they feared the show would fail. Was its jazz music the wrong choice? Why didn't it have a laugh track? Why did it get so quiet at times? Did the Bible story fit in with funny comics? Would they get complaints from viewers?

A Charlie Brown Christmas premiered on December 9, 1965. Almost half of the TV watchers in the United States viewed it! They loved the heartwarming story. It won an Emmy Award. When Sparky accepted the award he said,

"Charlie Brown is not used to winning, so we thank you."

A Charlie Brown Christmas is the longest-running TV cartoon special ever. It opens with an ice-skating scene. Skating was something Sparky and his family missed about Minnesota. When the ice rink in Santa Rosa, California, near the Schulzes' home closed, Sparky's wife, Joyce, oversaw the building of a new one. It was called the Redwood Empire Ice Arena. It opened in 1969 and is still located across from the Charles M. Schulz Museum and Research Center.

By 1971—just twenty-one years after the
first *Peanuts* comic appeared—the strip had one
hundred million readers! Sadly, Sparky and his
wife were divorced in 1972. This made him feel
like a failure. For a while, he drew his comics in
a room at the ice arena. He would eat breakfast
there at the Warm Puppy Café. Soon he built a
new office for himself called One Snoopy Place
just a short walk from the arena.

While his office was in the arena, Sparky met a woman there named Jean Forsyth Clyde. She was smart, lively, and interesting. He and Jean married in 1973.

Jean Forsyth Clyde

Sparky had fun in his free time playing cards with friends, hanging out with his dog, Andy, and playing sports like ice hockey and golf. He made his first and only hole in one at age seventy-two. That means he hit a ball from a tee to land in a faraway cup on the golf course in a single shot!

In *Peanuts,* Charlie Brown's little sister Sally has a crush on Linus. She says he's her "sweet babboo." That's a nickname Jean called Sparky. Sparky was in love and Jean adored him. He was happy, as happy as he could be.

Charles M. Schulz Museum
and Research Center

At the Charles M. Schulz Museum and Research Center in Santa Rosa, California, you can see a re-creation of Sparky's studio. His ink pens, his desk, and the drawing board where he drew *Peanuts* are set up like they were in his office at One Snoopy Place. Remember, Snoopy likes to write stories. They usually begin, "It was a dark and stormy night . . ." So one exhibit offers a chance to continue writing Snoopy's story. On the wall, visitors can display the page they write. They can also draw cartoons in the Education Room and watch documentaries in the Theater about the illustrator and his work. Best of all, the museum has the biggest collection of original *Peanuts* art in the world!

The label on the building reads: CHARLES M. SCHULZ MUSEUM AND RESEARCH CENTER

CHAPTER 10
Still Nuts for *Peanuts*

By the end of 1999, Sparky's comic strip was being printed in more than 2,600 newspapers worldwide. About 355 million people in 75 countries were reading it daily.

Fans had grown to love the *Peanuts* characters.

They felt almost like real friends. When Charlie Brown didn't get any valentines on Valentine's Day in the comic strip, readers mailed lots of valentines for him to Charles Schulz. Sometimes he was surprised that readers cared so much about his comic strip characters. But it was satisfying.

There have been forty-five animated *Peanuts* TV specials, a TV show, a miniseries, documentaries, and five movies. The *Peanuts* characters have appeared on the covers of national US magazines such as *Time, Life, Newsweek,* and *TV Guide.* Lucy and her lemonade stand appeared on the cover of *Ms.* magazine highlighting a story on how women could start their own businesses.

World-famous museums such as the Louvre in Paris and the Smithsonian in Washington, DC, have hosted *Peanuts*-themed exhibits. The first *Peanuts* products—plastic dolls—were sold in 1958. There are now over twenty thousand products based on the characters. Everything from greeting cards to pajamas to board games. An ice-skating Snoopy, a kite-flying Charlie Brown, and other *Peanuts* character balloons have been part of the Macy's Thanksgiving Day Parade in New York City.

Charles Schulz died in Santa Rosa, California, on February 12, 2000, at age seventy-seven. The next day his final comic strip appeared in the Sunday newspaper with a thank-you to his fans. In all, he had created 17,897 *Peanuts* comic strips (15,391 daily and 2,506 Sunday). He had worked hard to fulfill his dream and keep it going for fifty years.

Charles had drawn every one of the newspaper comic strips himself. In his last one, he wrote, "My family does not wish *Peanuts* to be continued by anyone else . . ." The daily comics he had already created, however, continue running in many newspapers.

Charles Schulz once said, "The only thing I ever wanted to be was a cartoonist. That's my life. Drawing."

Timeline of Charles Schulz's Life

1922 — Charles M. Schulz is born in Minneapolis, Minnesota

1937 — His drawing of the family dog, Spike, is published in a newspaper

1939 — Begins classes at Federal Schools

1942 — Drafted to fight in World War II in Europe

1943 — His mom dies

1947 — *Li'l Folks* cartoon is published in the *St. Paul Pioneer Press*

1950 — The first *Peanuts* comic strip is published

1951 — Marries Joyce Steele Halverson

1952 — *Peanuts* first appears in the Sunday funnies

1965 — *Peanuts* makes the cover of *Time* magazine

1968 — The first Black character (Franklin) appears in *Peanuts*

1969 — Apollo 10 modules named *Snoopy* and *Charlie Brown* blast into outer space

1973 — Marries Jean Forsyth Clyde

1996 — Gets a star on the Hollywood Walk of Fame

2000 — Dies on February 12. His last *Peanuts* comic appears in newspapers the next day

2002 — Awarded a Congressional Gold Medal

— The Charles M. Schulz Museum and Research Center opens in Santa Rosa, California

Timeline of the World

1927 — Babe Ruth hits sixty home runs in one season

1928 — *Steamboat Willie* cartoon starring Mickey Mouse hits theaters

1929 — The Wall Street stock market crashes

1930 — Mahatma Gandhi leads a 241-mile march in India to protest British rule

1939 — The New York World's Fair opens

1941 — The US joins European Allies in World War II

1951 — The NFL Championship Game is first shown on TV

1952 — Elizabeth II becomes queen of Great Britain and Northern Ireland

1953 — Edmund Hillary and Tenzing Norgay are the first to reach the summit of Mount Everest

1961 — The Berlin Wall goes up

1968 — Rev. Dr. Martin Luther King Jr. is assassinated

1969 — The Woodstock outdoor music festival is held

1981 — Sandra Day O'Connor becomes the first female US Supreme Court justice

1986 — A nuclear accident occurs at the Chernobyl power station in the Soviet Union

1989 — Chinese students protest for democracy in Beijing

2001 — Apple Inc. introduces the first iPod

Bibliography

*Books for young readers

*Gherman, Beverly. *Sparky: The Life and Art of Charles Schulz*.
San Francisco: Chronicle Books, 2010.

Inge, M. Thomas, ed. *Charles M. Schulz: Conversations*. Jackson,
MS: University Press of Mississippi, 2000.

Kidd, Chip. *Only What's Necessary: Charles M. Schulz and the
Art of Peanuts*. New York: Abrams ComicArts, 2015.

Mendelson, Lee. *A Boy Named Charlie Brown*. Santa Rosa, CA:
Peanuts Television, 1963. DVD.

Michaelis, David. *Schulz and Peanuts*. New York: Harper, 2007.

*Schulz, Charles M. *Meet the Peanuts Gang!* Adapted by Natalie
Shaw. New York: Simon Spotlight, 2015.

Schulz, Charles M. *My Life with Charlie Brown*. Jackson, MS:
University Press of Mississippi, 2010.

Websites

www.schulzmuseum.org

You can see *Peanuts* comics here:

www.gocomics.com/peanuts